BUSINESS BREAKTHROUGH STRATEGIES
FOR SOLOPRENEURS

How I Can Increase Your Revenue By $10k to $50k In Less Than 45 Minutes

Dr. Teresa R. Martin

Business Compliance & Breakthrough Expert

PUBLISHED BY BLUE ARTISTS, LLC

CONTENTS

How I Find $10k in 45 Minutes for Solopreneurs

The purpose of this book is to walk you through a process I've created where I can find any business a minimum of $10,000 in just 45 minutes.

I will go through 8 simple strategies that are proven revenue generators for any small business. Most business owners know nothing about these strategies, and therefore, are failing to capitalize on their revenue-generating power.

For the purposes of this book, I'll cover each of the 8 strategies in individual chapters for one main reason. I want you to be able to review these strategies and minimize the amount of time it will take you to implement them in their entirety.

But consider this… business owners today are in the fight of their lives. The global economy is in shambles, they have no additional revenue sources they can tap into for financial support during lean times… and perhaps worst of all, marketing and advertising just don't work as well as they used to. In fact, for many small business owners, marketing isn't producing any results for them at all… and their financial situation is growing more desperate by the day.

As a business owner or entrepreneur, if you're struggling right now to generate more leads and clients for your business, and you need to find immediate ways to dramatically increase your businesses bottom line revenue, then spend the next few minutes with me and I'll show you how I can help you make all of these problems disappear forever.

Small business owners today are desperate for proven and tested ways they can generate more leads, attract more clients and make more money. So what if I told you that I can show you how to generate all the leads a business owner needs in order to completely dominate their market? What if I could prove to you right now that I can make ANY small business owner more than $10,000 in additional revenue… and do it in just 30 days?

Over the next few minutes, I'm going to give you back door access to a series of powerful business growth strategies that are some of the most powerful revenue-generating strategies ever created.

So let's get started.

Chapter 1
More Leads – Marketing and Advertising

Let's face it. The major hot button for most small businesses these days is the ability to generate leads. All small businesses want more leads, but few of them know how to successfully attract customers to their business.

As a coach, I have in-depth knowledge and skill when it comes to generating leads. So here's the process I use to do this.

If you're like 99% of the business owners I speak with, you may often feel lost or overwhelmed as you try to navigate through all the various options available these days. Websites, social media, SEO, email marketing, Facebook, pay-per-click and so on.

Let me do you a favor right now and completely remove that overwhelm from your life forever. Are you familiar with the 80/20 rule?

For business owners, it means that 20% of what you do every day is generating 80% of your total annual revenue.

In other words, you're only doing a few things daily that makes you most of your money. I can tell you specifically what makes up that 20%, and that's all you really need to focus on after today.

There are 5 areas that make up that 20%... leads, conversions, transactions, pricing and profits.

Remember I told you that I'm going to find you more than $10,000 in less than 45 minutes today?

I'm going to do that by focusing on just 2 or 3 of these 5 areas... so you can imagine what you could actually generate revenue-wise if you implemented all 5 areas.

In fact, let me show you what's possible, and why these 5 areas are so critical.

I use a tool called a Profit Growth Calculator. Do you by chance know the exact number of leads and sales you've made over the past 12 months?

No! That's OK... let's plug in numbers for a make believe business. Let's say your business generated 1000 leads in the past year... and your average conversion rate was 25%.

Let's also say your customers bought what you sell 10 times throughout the year... and they typically paid on average around $100 per purchase.

Finally, let's say your profit margin per sale is only 25%.

Notice at the bottom that you're earning $62,500 annually. But look what happens if we simply increase each of these 5 areas by a meager 10%.

You would see your annual revenue almost double... from $62,500 to over 6 figures. By the way, that's the ballpark most business coaches play in... the 10% increase range. Nothing wrong with that either, believe me.

Most business owners would KILL to almost double their revenue, wouldn't you agree? But watch what happens if you could increase each of the 5 areas by 50%.

Your business would skyrocket from $62,500 to almost half a million dollars annually. Now, you may be thinking that 50% gains in each of these 5 areas would be next to impossible. Let

THE
PROFIT GROWTH CALCULATOR

	Baseline	10% Increase	50% Increase
1 More Leads	1000	1100.00	
Input number of annual leads E.g. 1000			
2 More Conversions	25 %	27.5%	
Input annual conversion rate percentage E.g. 25%			
Customers: 250		302	
3 More Transactions	10	11.00	
Input number of annual transactions per individual customer E.g. 10			
4 Higher Prices	$ 100	110.00	
Input average dollar amount of each customer transaction E.g. 100			
Total Revenue: $250,000.00		$365,420.00	
5 More Profits	25 %	27.5%	
Input annual profit as a percentage E.g. 25%			
Profit: $62,500.00		$100,490.50	

me assure you that a 50% increase is child's play, and I'm going to prove it to you right now.

When you completed my mini-audit for your business, I noticed that when I asked you what marketing materials you have to promote your business... you said none. May I ask how you're currently generating leads?

Most business owners tell me "word of mouth" or more often than not... "referrals." Referrals are obviously an excellent lead source. In fact, it may be the best one by far, but the problem is you never know when you will get them. They're not reliable... and you certainly can't generate them whenever you want.

99% of businesses today do have a website. Do you know for sure how many leads your website generates every month? Do you know for sure how many sales your website produces every month?

Can I show you why your website isn't generating leads or closing sales for you? In fact, would you like for me to give you the deeply hidden secrets that the marketing guru's DON'T want you to know?

Here's the key to successful marketing. You MUST be able to enter the conversation taking place in the head of your prospects. Or another way to look at it is to be able to address the number one question on your prospects mind at just the right time. So how do you do this? It's actually quite simple when you know and understand the fundamentals of marketing.

The conversation that's taking place in EVERY prospect's mind revolves around two major points. There's a problem they have and they don't want... and there's a result they want but don't have.

Now believe it or not, there is actually a marketing formula we follow that takes these two points into account... and spits out a message so compelling it practically forces your prospects to buy what you sell.

It's called the Conversion Equation, and it looks like this... Interrupt, Engage, Educate and Offer. The Interrupt is your headline – which means it's the first thing someone sees when they visit your website, read any of your marketing collateral... or hear you speak. When someone asks you what you do, it's the first words out of your mouth. That's your headline... and it MUST address the problem your prospects have that they don't want.

The Engage is your subheadline – which is the second thing your prospects see or hear. It MUST address the result your prospect wants but doesn't have. The Educate is the information you provide... either verbally or in writing... that presents evidence to your prospects that you and your product or service are superior in every way to your competition.

Unfortunately, MOST businesses aren't different from their competitors, and that's why you MUST innovate your business to create what we refer to as a market-dominating position.

You MUST make your business unique... it MUST stand out from the crowd. It MUST make your prospects say to themselves that they would be absolute idiots to buy from anyone else but you – regardless of price. And finally, the Offer. You MUST create a compelling offer that makes it so irresistible your prospects can't turn it down. But here's another critical fundamental of marketing.

Because of the saturation of marketing messaging these days, most prospects have become numb to most marketing.

Following our Conversion Equation can dramatically overcome this, but even with this powerful tool in play, it will still take multiple "touch" points before your prospects will buy what you sell.

For most businesses today, it takes anywhere from 20 to more than 100 touch points before a prospect makes their buying decision. Following the Conversion Equation reduces the touch points to somewhere between 5 to 12 points of contact.

But here's the key... most businesses don't follow up with their prospects at all, and this provides a HUGE window of opportunity for ANY business that does follow up... to position themselves as the dominant force in their industry.

But in order to have the opportunity to get your message in front of your prospects 5 to 12 times, you MUST find a way to collect their contact information, and that's the purpose of your Offer.

Most businesses offer something that only appeals to prospects we call NOW buyers... prospects ready to make an immediate purchase. Unfortunately, NOW buyers make up less than 1% of the total number of prospects that are in the market to buy what you sell.

These businesses typically offer prospects a free consultation, a discount, a coupon, a free assessment, a complimentary quote... or the biggest mistake of all... CALL US!

For most businesses, all of their marketing material... their website... their business card... all list their phone number as their sole offer... and that ONLY appeals to that 1% of NOW buyers. The remaining 99% of viable prospects are "investigating" and gathering information about what you sell.

They're searching for information because they want to determine who is offering the best value. You see, prospects DON'T shop price – they shop VALUE!

The only reason prospects consider price is that most businesses don't give them any other value proposition to consider except price.

Remember what I said a moment ago about making your business unique – creating a market-dominating position?

Most businesses don't do that, and since they... and all of their competitors... look exactly the same, prospects are FORCED to shop price. So with these fundamentals in mind, let's see how your website stacks up to them.

Let me show you a website we just revised for a child psychologist so you can see what I mean... and then let's take a look at your website as a comparison. Here is the child psychologist's original website.

This is typical for this profession, and 99% of his colleagues' websites look EXACTLY like this. Notice the generic headline... Parenting Advice and Resources from Dr. John Smith.

He has to have a headline like that because he's attempting to be all things to all prospects. Basically, this doctor helps parents deal with adolescent problems. Look at the 9 areas he services... emotionally disturbed kids, behavioral problems, teen pregnancy, peer pressure and so on.

So let's compare this site with the fundamentals we just discussed. First, you MUST create a market-dominating position. This doctor could actually create 9 of them by simply positioning his specialty in each of his 9 individual areas of treatment.

For example, let's say he decides to start with the top condition on his list... emotionally disturbed kids. These are kids that yell, scream and constantly have a highly belligerent attitude toward their parents. They scream at them and are known in some cases to threaten the parents. These kids can't be reasoned with... and these poor parents have NO clue how to deal with this situation.

So here's what this doctor needs to do. Forget the website completely – this doctor needs what we call a squeeze page. This is a single page that's online... and that specifically addresses ONLY this one condition. So what should this page look like... and what should it say?

Remember the second fundamental – you MUST enter the conversation taking place in the head of your prospect. There's a problem they have that they don't want... and there's a result they want but they don't have. This is where we implement the first two components of the Conversion Equation... Interrupt and Engage. The headline is the Interrupt and it must address the problem they have and don't want.

Here's the squeeze page we created for this doctor that did that.

Notice the headline… Are You Sick And Tired Of The Yelling, Screaming And Belligerent Attitude Of Your Child? Does that address the problem these parents have and they don't want? Would you say that's a 100% bullseye?

Now for the Engage which is the subheadline. It MUST address the result they want but they don't have. Notice it says… Now You Can Discover The Secrets To Controlling Your Child And Instantly Restore Peace And Quiet In Your Home. Would you say that's bullseye number two?

Now let's look at the third Conversion Equation component... Educate. In the doctor's original website, because he's trying to appeal to all prospects, his video said this. Greeting parents. I want to welcome you to remarkable parenting. You will find tons of great information here... with hundreds of pages of articles.

Think how ridiculous this sounds if I'm one of these parents with a kid that has a belligerent attitude. Do I want to read hundreds of pages of articles? Or am I searching for a specific solution to a specific problem? Do you see why most websites these days are basically a total and complete waste of money? They don't address the things your prospects are truly looking for. Here's the new script we created for this doctor.

"As a parent, are you struggling to gain control of your child's attitude and emotions? Is your child yelling and screaming at you, while often displaying a belligerent and sometimes threatening tone that no matter what you do or try... you just can't seem to get under control?

My name is Dr. John Smith, and I help parents like you every day learn the techniques that will solve these frustrating and destructive behavioral patterns once and for all. In fact, let me prove it to you. Enter your first name and email in the box to the right, and I'll send you a series of 60 second techniques that will immediately restore peace and quiet in your home."

Think that just might get more prospects to respond to this message? And that brings us to the final component of the Conversion Equation... the Offer. Look at the doctor's original offer. It was for a free consultation. The only prospects that will accept that type of offer are those NOW buyers, and remember that they're less than 1% of the total number of prospects looking for this type of help.

When your offer is to "call me," that basically says "let me sell you" to your prospects. We are so used to getting non-stop sales pitches these days that we resist calling anyone with every fiber of our being. Most people these days won't answer their phone unless they recognize the caller ID. This type of offer is called an incentive offer, and incentive offers only work for common purchases, emergency situations and impulse purchases.

And remember, most prospects don't buy until they have been exposed to your messaging somewhere between 5 to 12 times. If you tell prospects to "call you," and most won't, how do you keep marketing to them? Obviously you can't. The secret to effective marketing is to offer what most prospects truly want... INFORMATION!

Look at the last sentence in the child psychologist's video script... "enter your first name and email in the box to the right, and I'll send you a series of 60 second techniques that will immediately restore peace and quiet in your home." That offer is ZERO risk to a prospect, and it offers them something they truly want... a solution to their problem.

They can receive it by simply providing their name and email address... WITHOUT having to speak to anyone... or be subjected to any type of sales pitch. That's why the offer on this doctor's squeeze page says... "Learn The Secrets To Gaining And Maintaining Complete Control Of Your Child In Less Than 60 Seconds." Is that a highly compelling offer that would appeal to a majority of the prospects directed to this page?

And do you now see why we call this a squeeze page? There are NO navigation buttons on this page to distract the prospect. In fact, there is only ONE action they can take... enter their contact information. Otherwise, they have to close the page completely... and if they do, THAT is when we can redirect them to the doctor's main website to see if there is something else that might grab their attention.

That informational offer provides them with proof that this doctor can actually get them the results they're looking for, and then within that information is an offer for them to schedule a consultation with the doctor, which they are now more likely to do.

But consider these numbers for this doctor's <u>original</u> website. He could easily generate 300 or more leads per month using a pay-per-click campaign on Facebook. Those leads are then sent to his original website. He will then average around 10% of those leads... or 30 prospects... will see his offer for the free consultation and will call to <u>inquire</u> about it.

Notice I said INQUIRE about it, NOT request it. Out of that 10% that will call... only 10% of them will actually consent to the consultation... which equals 3 prospects.

Fortunately for most professionals like this doctor, they typically convert 100% of the prospects they get in front of... so those 3 prospects will more than likely become patients. Note that out of 300 leads, the doctor winds up with 3 new clients. That is the national average today... 1% of all leads generated will typically convert into a new client. That's pathetic!

But now let's look at the doctor's new squeeze page. First of all, let's leave his number of leads at 300 per month. That squeeze page won't impact that number whatsoever. But let me ask you this, and give me your open and honest opinion.

Do you think this new page will increase the number of prospects that will request this doctor's secrets to gaining and maintaining complete control of their child? The doctor was getting 10% with his old site. What percent do you think would request this new, more compelling offer?

Most responses I get average somewhere between 50% to 70%. Well, suppose we stay really conservative and say that just 20% request the new offer.

That would mean 60 prospects would receive those secrets and actually see for themselves that this doctor's methods really work.

And once they do, what percent of those do you think might request the consultation with the doctor? Remember that originally it was just 10%.

Again, most responses I get average between 50% to 70%. I would tend to agree with those numbers, but we know he originally converted 10%, so to be really conservative, let's just leave that conversion rate the same... 10%.

So out of the 60 prospects requesting the doctor's secrets, 6 of them now request the consultation. And let's assume like we did originally that the doctor converts all 6 of them into patients. That's an additional 3 patients per month, isn't it?

Now let's say this doctor only charges $800 for his services, even though in reality it's typically 3 times that amount. $800 times 3 new patients is an additional $2,400 per month... which is an annual increase of $28,800. That's obviously a dramatic increase in revenue considering we're being ridiculously conservative... and all we did was make some slight changes to this doctor's site.

So let me ask you this. Do you think we could get similar results for your business? How many leads have you generated in the last 12 months?

How many leads would you estimate you've generated this month? Great, now how many of those leads requested your offer? If we could create a similar process for your business... and offer compelling information to your prospects just like we did for the child psychologist... do you think more prospects would respond? By what percent?

Could we <u>conservatively</u> agree that a 10% opt-in rate is easily a no brainer? So do you realize that just that one change alone would double your current sales revenue?

And that's assuming we don't increase your number of leads or your final conversion rate... which we will. If you said your last month's revenue was $25,000... then just this one change alone adds an additional $25,000 to your bottom line.

In a recent case study I conducted, I found **$58,000** in additional annual revenue just using this one simple strategy.

But consider this!

That additional revenue is NOT just a one-time increase. That's revenue that business will generate year after year after year.

And... **$58,000** in additional annual revenue increases the valuation of that business somewhere in the range of **$150,000 - $200,000**.

Chapter 2
More Leads – Joint Ventures

Do you currently have any established joint venture partnerships?

JV's involve two or more businesses that decide to form a partnership to share markets or endorse a specific product or service to their customer base… usually under a revenue share arrangement. The key to creating successful joint ventures is to find partners who service the exact same type of clients that need or want what you sell.

Let me give you an example and I'll use one we're both familiar with… a florist. One of the most financially lucrative product lines for a florist is providing flowers for weddings. The average floral bill for a wedding often exceeds $3,000. But what we discovered about florists is they fall into what we refer to as an "event chain." An event chain simply refers to a series of businesses that customers purchase from in a specific sequence.

For example, a wedding will never take place until an engagement ring is purchased from a jeweler. So jewelers are at the forefront of every wedding chain. Once the young lady accepts that engagement ring, this event chain kicks into high gear. First, this young lady knows EXACTLY where she wants to get married, so number one on her agenda is to book the church, chapel or synagogue where she wants the ceremony held.

Second on her list is to line up her wedding planner. Weddings today are a really big deal, and often women like to use the services of a professional wedding planner. Next up, she wants to secure the venue for her reception.

She knows most venues book out months in advance, so locking in that venue is high on her priority list. After that comes the wedding dress, so she begins the search for the perfect dress at an affordable price.

Next is our florist. The bride-to-be will want to begin selecting her floral arrangements for both the wedding and the reception. Then after the florist comes the wedding cake… the printer for the invitations and thank you cards… and depending on the financial ability of the bride to be, she may also be interested in hiring a limo… a DJ for the reception… a travel planner for the honeymoon… the hotel… catering and so on.

This event chain is typical of this industry. And for the florist, it specifically identifies a multitude of potential and very lucrative JV partners. But here's why this becomes so important.

Every business ABOVE the florist has the potential to ENDORSE and SEND prospects to the florist. Unfortunately, the florist has NO control over that flow of prospects. Every business above the florist controls the JV relationship, so it's critical the florist create such a compelling offer and relationship with these businesses that they feel <u>obligated</u> to send prospects their way.

But here's what's even better. The <u>florist</u> controls the prospect flow to ALL the businesses BELOW them in the chain, and by establishing specific processes and procedures to make sure their customers use those businesses, the florist can negotiate compelling offers with those business owners as well. So consider these numbers.

Let's say this florist cultivates a JV relationship with at least one of each business throughout this entire chain. Staying ultra-

conservative with our estimates, would you agree this florist...
since they have NO control over the flow of prospects from
these businesses... is it likely they could obtain at least ONE
referral each month from just <u>one</u> of the businesses above
them?

OK, would you also agree conservatively that since the <u>florist</u>
controls the flow of prospects to the businesses BELOW
them... that they could easily send at least ONE referral to
EACH one of them every month? Keep in mind these are
VERY conservative estimates we're using here.

Since the average floral bill for a wedding is $3,000... then just
ONE referral per month from those businesses ABOVE the
florist increases their <u>annual</u> revenue by $36,000. Now let's
consider the businesses BELOW the florist where the <u>florist</u>
controls the referrals. Let's start with the wedding cake maker.

The average sales price for a wedding cake is also $3,000, and
the florist could easily negotiate a 10% referral fee. So just a
<u>single</u> referral per month produces an additional annual
increase of $3,600 for the florist.

Now consider the printer. The average sales price for printing
is $1,000, and the florist again could receive a 10% referral fee,

so that <u>single</u> referral per month produces an additional annual increase of $1,200.

If we stop there, this florist has just increased their annual revenue by more than $40,000... and that's using ridiculously conservative numbers. Imagine if you continued to add up the revenue produced by all the additional referral fees the florist would earn from all the other vendors in this chain.

This same process holds true for businesses that aren't in a chain. But just like the florist, they simply identify partners who service the exact same <u>type</u> of clients that need or want what they sell. Now I realize this looks easy, but it's not... and here's why.

You not only have to properly identify who would make an excellent joint venture partner for your business... but you also must determine the order to approach each one... how to approach them... and when to approach them. It's critical you do this properly or you wind up burning through all of your potential JV partners and come out with nothing in return.

Let me ask you a quick question. Just off the top of your head, how many potential JV partners would you estimate might be a fit for what you sell? Would you believe that I've identified more than a dozen for your profession? So conservatively, how many referrals would you estimate might be possible if a dozen other businesses were compelled to refer their customers to you for additional purchases?

Conservatively, let's say you only get 3 referrals every month that buy from you. That's less than one per week. How much additional revenue would that add monthly? Now multiply that by 12 to see your annual revenue increase.

One more thing before we move on. Remember earlier we discussed the critical importance of creating a highly compelling informational offer that would promise so much value to prospects that they would knock your door down to get it?

Suppose the florist offered this informational offer in their marketing… "5 Things Every Bride Should Know To Avoid Disaster On Their Wedding Day." This offer would place TONS of prospects into their drip campaign and result in a tremendous increase in sales. Those new sales can then be referred to their new JV partners and they collect multiple referral fees every month.

This would absolutely dwarf the revenue we just uncovered for the florist in this example. What I find really exciting about JV's is this is a strategy I help my clients implement immediately…

and it begins generating instant cash flow for them right out of the gate.

In a recent case study I conducted, I found $65,000 in additional annual revenue just using the JV strategy.

And again, that's revenue that business will generate year after year after year.

$65,000 in additional annual revenue increases the valuation of that business somewhere in the range of $195,000 - $260,000.

Chapter 3
More Conversions –
Downselling

So far we've only discussed 2 different lead generation strategies. Now let's discuss 2 lead <u>conversion</u> strategies… and let's start with downselling. Do you currently use a downsell strategy?

Downselling is nothing more than offering a prospect an alternative at a lower price when they decline your original offer. The goal is to turn the prospect into a client so you not only realize some short term financial benefit... but you gain the opportunity to do business with them again in the future.

For example, local health clubs always try to sell new members a full one year membership. If that fails, they will try to downsell them by offering a 90 day "health makeover" membership. If that fails, they may go to a 30 day or possibly a one week "trial" membership. They know if they can just get them to buy something the odds of them staying with them long term goes up exponentially.

Consider the florist. Most guys show up at a florist to buy roses for their better half. Valentine's Day, her birthday, their anniversary, Mother's Day and so on. But suppose a dozen roses cost $50 and the guy doesn't have that much money to spend. Since he has flowers on his mind, do you think he would consider an alternative that was just as romantic?

Do you realize if the alternative cost only $25, and that florist only used that downsell once each day which is highly conservative, that would add almost $8,000 in annual revenue for them? And that's just one possible downsell opportunity. Suppose they had floral alternatives for weddings, lower priced options for funerals and so on.

What's your current price point for what you currently sell? Think you could come up with an alternative for half that price? How many of those would you conservatively estimate you could sell each week? Now multiply your reduced price times your number of weekly sales… then multiply that number times 52 weeks to reveal your annual increase.

And that's just one downsell. How many additional downsell opportunities would you conservatively estimate you could easily develop?

I recently found a business owner $65,000 in additional annual revenue through targeted downselling... and that additional revenue continues to grow year after year.

$65,000 in additional annual revenue increases the valuation of that business somewhere in the range of $200,000 - $230,000.

Chapter 4
More Conversions – Drip Campaign

When a prospect doesn't buy what you sell, how many times do you follow up with them?

Small business owners focus primarily on generating leads. But remember that on average, less than 1% of prospects are NOW buyers. 99% are NOT ready to purchase that day, but many of them will buy sometime in the future... IF you continue to nurture them by staying in touch on an on-going basis.

Unfortunately, the vast majority of small business owners rarely if ever follow up with their prospects after their <u>initial</u> contact with them. So why is that important? Listen to this VERY carefully! 80% + of <u>ALL</u> sales occur between the 5th and the

12th point of contact between the business and the prospect. 80%!!! Are you starting to see an opportunity here? This is where you need to implement a "drip campaign."

A drip campaign can add significant revenue to your business. It automatically delivers a form of communication to customers or prospects on a predetermined and scheduled basis. But here's the really cool part about this. Once you create your compelling offer, all you have to do is take specific segments from that offer and send it to your prospects on a consistent basis.

Let me show you an example of how this was done for a client that owned a sunroom company. When homeowners consider any type of remodeling project... whether it's their kitchen, an updated bathroom... or in this case, installing a sunroom... wouldn't they love to get their hands on what you might call an "Idea Guide" that features various models or state-of-the-art concepts?

Let me show you the Idea Guide that was developed for this sunroom company.

7 Benefits
Of Owning A Sunroom

If I have heard it once, I have heard it a thousand times... "what was I thinking, I should have added my sunroom years ago". Almost every client we work with at Costal Empire Exteriors, is absolutely amazed at the increase in the quality of life they experience after adding a sunroom. It may be hard to believe, so let me see if I can quantify for you the benefits of owning a sunroom and keep in mind - these benefit idea statements come directly from our clients.

Benefit #1 -
Enjoy The Outdoors 365 Days A Year
Ever been stuck inside on a rainy day, wishing you could be sitting outside hearing the patter of the rain and watching the lighting without getting soaked? Ever see the snow fall and want to be in the middle of it without freezing or getting frostbite? How about sit outside on a sunny day and watch the birds, or the flowers blow in the wind without sweating or getting burned by the sun? A sunroom allows you to extend your home "into nature" in a safe and comfortable way. It allows you to move your backyard "into" your home without the insects, dirt, grime and other nuisances.

Benefit #4 –
Recharge Your Solar Batteries

More and more documented studies are beginning to prove what your mother and grandmother always knew… getting an appropriate amount of sunshine on your skin every few days provides vital nutrients, vitamins and minerals that the human body needs.

The problem has always been that to get sun meant you had to be outside – which means you are at the mercy of Mother Nature. Bugs, hot weather and even the occasional windy day all make recharging the batteries a pain sometimes.

With a sunroom, you get to control the temperature, you get to eliminate pests like ants, flies, mosquitoes and other nuisances – and wind is a non issue. You can sit in your sun room, at a comfortable 73 degrees while getting a full healthy exposure to the sun.

Benefit #5 –
Increase The Value Of Your Home

If you have plans to sell your home in the next 3-7 years and want to really see a huge return on investment, add a sunroom. Putting in even a small sunroom can increase the value of a home by %30-%120. I am sure you could agree that if you were looking for a home and found 2 options, one with a sunroom and one without – you would try and get the home with the sunroom.

Besides the added square feet to the home, it adds a uniqueness that is likely not found in your neighborhood currently. It also adds a general appeal that almost no one can turn down. Its rather amazing to dig into the statistics showing how fast and for how much more homes with sunrooms sell compared to homes without.

Master Bedroom Sunroom — This type of sunroom isn't for everyone, as it can be really bright in the morning, but for those early risers who enjoy the progressive light of the sun or enjoy opening the shades in the sunroom early in the morning to capture those first morning rays - this is the room for you. If you are an early riser you will be amazed at just how easy it is to rise with a sunroom 10 feet from your bed. You can wake up, walk over, pray, meditate or just relax while reading the paper. Size wise it falls into the medium category and is one of the least common types of sunrooms we find in homes today.

Back Porch Sunroom — Probably the most commonly thought about type of sunroom, and the most practical. It sits at the back of the home and adds a large amount of space to the home while providing a comfortable inviting sitting or relaxing area for when guests arrive or just for a nice quiet brunch with the spouse. Sometimes these will include a hot tub.

Pretty impressive, wouldn't you agree? Well, would you like to hear the sad thing about this type of informational offer? Most prospects don't read it. They will request it with every intention of reading it, but only about 20% of them actually will. That's Ok though, because it has already done its job… which was to compel the prospect to give us their contact information so we can begin our 5 to 12 touch points. And we simply use the information in the Idea Guide to do that quickly, efficiently and inexpensively.

Here are a few examples for the sunroom company.

Notice in the Idea Guide it starts out listing the 7 benefits of owning a sunroom. Benefit number one – enjoy the outdoors 365 days a year. Obviously that's a HUGE reason someone would buy a sunroom, but unfortunately, 80% of prospects won't read that. So let's reintroduce that benefit in our drip campaign and drive it home to the prospect. This sunroom company did that using a 6 X 11 oversized postcard, but they could have also done it through email.

Here's the postcard they sent out that emphasized this benefit.

Notice that benefit number 4 says that owning a sunroom
recharges your solar batteries.

Benefit #4 –
Recharge Your Solar Batteries
More and more documented studies are
beginning to prove what your mother
and grandmother always knew... getting
an appropriate amount of sunshine on
your skin every few days provides vital
nutrients, vitamins and minerals that the
human body needs.

The problem has always been that to
get sun meant you had to be outside –
which means you are at the mercy
of Mother Nature. Bugs, hot weather
and even the occasional windy day all
make recharging the batteries a pain
sometimes.

With a sunroom, you get to control the
temperature, you get to eliminate pests
like ants, flies, mosquitoes and other
nuisances – and wind is a non issue. You
can sit in your sun room, at a
comfortable 73 degrees while getting a
full healthy exposure to the sun.

Benefit #5 –
Increase The Value
Of Your Home
If you have plans to sell your home in the
next 3-7 years and want to really see a huge
return on investment, add a sunroom.
Putting in even a small sunroom can
increase the value of a home by %50-%120.
I am sure you could agree that if you were
looking for a home and found 2 options,
one with a sunroom and one without – you
would try and get the home with the
sunroom.

Besides the added square feet to the home,
it adds a uniqueness that is likely not
found in your neighborhood currently. It
also adds a general appeal that almost no
one can turn down. It's rather amazing to
dig into the statistics showing how fast and
for how much more homes with sunrooms
sell compared to homes without.

Here's the postcard that emphasizes that benefit.

Benefit number 5 is major as it educates prospects that a sunroom actually increases the value of their home. So this postcard reinforces that fact.

But my point in showing you these is to emphasize that once you create your compelling informational offer, you pretty much have everything you need to implement your drip campaign. But look what begins to happen from the first day you start your drip campaign.

Let me go back to the child psychologist to show you the true impact of a drip campaign. If the child psychologist generated 300 leads per month, conservatively speaking we said he would average 60 prospects that would opt-in for his informational offer… and of those that did… 6 of those 60 would become patients of his. So that means 54 prospects did NOT buy his services.

Those are the prospects that now begin receiving the doctor's drip campaign. Out of those 54 prospects, an additional 2 of them will typically buy in the next 30 days. This is a pattern that continues month after month for as long as the doctor continues to stay in touch with these prospects… and continues to offer them value. Every month 54 new prospects go into the top of the doctor's "funnel," and 2 additional sales per 54 prospects continues to be delivered from the bottom of the funnel.

Here's what the numbers look like over the first year.

54

54 + 52

54 + 52 + 50

54 + 52 + 50 + 48

54 + 52 + 50 + 48 + 46

54 + 52 + 50 + 48 + 46 + 44

54 + 52 + 50 + 48 + 46 + 44 + 42

54 + 52 + 50 + 48 + 46 + 44 + 42 + 40

54 + 52 + 50 + 48 + 46 + 44 + 42 + 40 + 38

54 + 52 + 50 + 48 + 46 + 44 + 42 + 40 + 38 + 36

54 + 52 + 50 + 48 + 46 + 44 + 42 + 40 + 38 + 36 + 34

54 + 52 + 50 + 48 + 46 + 44 + 42 + 40 + 38 + 36 + 34 + 32

At the end of year one, the doctor will have generated 4080 new prospects… and 72 new clients through his squeeze page. But then the doctor produced a staggering 156 new clients through his drip campaign. And that's just year one!

This growth pattern continues year after year for as long as the doctor maintains this sales process. But here's the problem. By month 12 of year one, the doctor is generating 30 NEW patients every month. Is that a number this doctor can handle logistically? There's a limit on the number of patients this doctor can reasonable handle, and when that number is reached, this doctor can literally STOP ALL lead generation efforts and let his drip campaign continue to produce additional patients far into the future.

Now let's calculate how this strategy will conservatively impact YOUR business. Remember, 80% of sales take place only AFTER 5 to 12 points of contact…and NONE of your competitors are doing anything like this whatsoever. Since you will be the only one in your market with this in place, you can logically expect to see a dramatic increase in both sales and conversions.

However, for the purpose of today's exercise, let's stay extremely conservative and calculate just a 10% conversion rate for your drip campaign. What was your total sales revenue last year? Whatever your number is… take 10% of that total. That's an ultra-conservative estimate of what a drip campaign can easily produce for your business over the next 12 months… and that conservative amount can easily double each year… year after year… for as long as you keep your drip campaign in place. That's pretty exciting, isn't it?

During a recent business assessment, I found $75,000 in additional annual revenue by implementing a simple drip campaign… and that grows exponentially year after year.

$75,000 in additional annual revenue increases the valuation of that business somewhere in the range of $225,000 - $300,000.

Chapter 5
More Transactions – Upsell / Cross-sell

Let's move on to our third profit formula area. This involves increasing transactions with your prospects. In other words, getting them to buy from you more frequently than they do now. There are 2 powerful revenue generating strategies that will work here.

Are you familiar with upselling and cross-selling? When you go to McDonald's and the kid behind the counter asks if you would like your meal "supersized," that's upselling. When that same kid then asks if you would like an apple pie to go with your supersized meal, that's cross-selling.

Upselling means offering a higher grade or quality or size of the item that the customer may be interested in at the point when the customer is ready to buy. Cross-selling means offering other products or services which <u>complement</u> the item the customer is interested in, at the point when the customer is ready to buy.

Now here's what most business owners don't realize. 34% of prospects will buy additional products or services at the time of their original purchase… IF they're asked to do so. Most businesses NEVER ask them, and they lose out on this lucrative opportunity to dramatically increase their revenue. Let me show you a brilliant example of this.

Up until about 3 years ago, most car owners on average paid around $29 to get their oil changed. Today, you can get your oil changed all day long for around $10. Take a look at this Groupon that was recently offered for 3 oil changes plus 3 additional services of your choice per visit.

The price for these today averages around $18. That's $6 per oil change… and then they add on an additional $4.50 for oil disposal, so the total for each oil change is less than $11. That's obviously a bargain. So why do they offer this when they used to get $29?

Simple… they finally realized the power of upselling and cross-selling, and they can't get the opportunity to upsell or cross-sell if they don't get themselves in <u>front</u> of their prospects. This Groupon is designed for <u>one</u> purpose only… to get them in front of as many prospects as possible… and the best way to do that is to give them what are basically free services.

But here's what most businesses don't understand about this strategy. This Econo Lube is breaking even by offering this Groupon. That $11 covers their material and labor costs. And those 8 free services you see listed along the bottom… you can select any 3 of them per visit… because Econo Lube is going to perform all of those services anyway. They know they make most of their profit through their higher dollar service offerings, like batteries, brakes, transmission services and repairs.

So after the technician changes your oil, they're going to take all of your tires off so they can inspect your brakes… and cross-sell you a brake job. Since they have to remove all your tires to do that, why not offer you free tire rotation and a free brake inspection. Most of their patrons have no idea they're going to do this anyway, so they have this perception they're receiving all these services that they normally have to pay to have done… for free!

Notice Econo Lube offers to do a complete vehicle trip check where they do a complete inspection of your car before you take a long trip. A dealership would charge around $100 for that service, but Econo Lube includes 2 of these every 12 months. Well of course… they want to do this. I guarantee you that after checking over your entire vehicle, they WILL find SOMETHING wrong with your car. And since you're leaving on an extended trip, you will naturally want them to fix everything that's wrong. Are you starting to see the brilliance of this strategy?

So the key takeaway here for this strategy is to get yourself in front of your prospects as often as you can so you give yourself more opportunities to sell them more. So let me show you how this exact same strategy will work for a dentist. Obviously a dentist is about as far from an Econo Lube as you can get, but the principle is exactly the same… get in front of prospects and upsell / cross-sell them.

A dentist offers basic dental services like exams and teeth cleaning. That is NOT where they make their money. A dentist generates the vast majority of their revenue from cosmetic services, root canals, crowns, fillings and braces. So obviously the more patients they can get in front of, the more of these services they sell. The problem for dentists is that most people already have a dentist, and 90% of them will never change unless their dentist either retires or dies.

So what might convince someone to leave their current dentist? Consider these stats… 85% of the population have medical insurance, but only 50% have dental insurance. Among those without dental insurance, 44% said that was the main reason they didn't visit the dentist. See an opportunity here if you're a dentist?

What do you think might happen if a dentist specifically targeted families <u>without</u> dental insurance… and offered them virtually the exact same services as those <u>with</u> dental insurance… but <u>without</u> paying the expensive monthly premiums? Here's a marketing campaign that was designed to do this for a dentist in Richardson, Texas.

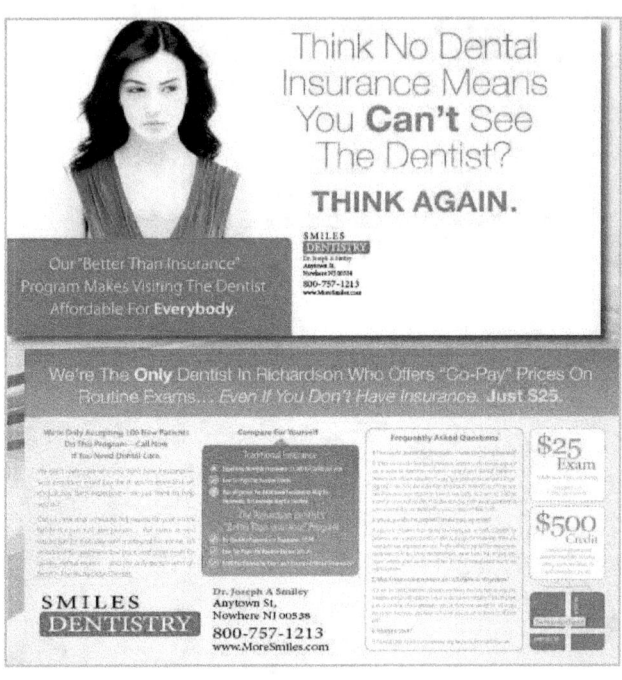

This obviously exploded this dentists' practice, but you might be thinking... how could he afford to offer this type of program? Same way the Econo Lube did!

The dentist basically offered patients routine services at his cost. That $25 covered the labor cost for the dental technician to take x-rays and clean the patient's teeth. But the dentist now had double the patients to upsell and cross-sell his more expensive and profitable services to. And of course, any business can always resort to the standard way to upsell and cross-sell customers... just make them more offers. A restaurant that was experiencing reduced revenue followed this advice.

They analyzed their profit margins on every one of their offerings, and determined their highest profit margin offerings were wine, appetizers and desserts. They literally doubled their sales on all three of these by training the staff to offer them to every one of their patrons.

For example, they instructed their staff to bring an appetizer and wine cart to each table BEFORE the patrons ordered... and offer free individual samples. Then the staff repeated the same process at the end of each patron's meal by bringing the dessert cart around and giving a free sample of each dessert to everyone at the table as a way to entice patrons to order one of them. The taste and "reciprocity" instantly <u>doubled</u> their appetizer, wine and dessert sales. But they didn't stop there.

The restaurant dramatically increased its <u>total</u> order revenue by implementing an <u>initial</u> order upsell strategy with the wait staff. They trained the staff to describe the more expensive entrée's on the menu and give the patrons their personal recommendation. Most patrons have a tendency to go with the staff's recommendations… and this easily increased their total entree revenue by 15%.

So let's assign a revenue figure for this strategy to your business. Remember that even a mediocre business can expect to see a 34% revenue increase by implementing this strategy. But since we want to be extremely conservative in our estimates, let's just factor in a 10% increase for your business. What's 10% of your annual revenue? That's what you could add to the bottom line of your business immediately using this strategy.

Just recently, I found $30,000 in additional annual revenue through a targeted upsell / cross-sell campaign.

$30,000 in additional annual revenue increases the valuation of that business somewhere in the range of $90,000 - $120,000.

Chapter 6
More Transactions – Expand Product / Service Offerings

Next, let's look at our second strategy for increasing transactions, and discuss how you could expand the number of products and services you offer. If you already provide a quality product / service, your current customers will be open to a variety of items that you introduce, recommend or endorse to them. Look... your current customers trust you don't they? Then they will DEMAND additional products and services from you because they do trust you.

Unfortunately, most businesses don't have additional products or services to offer their client base, so you want to ask yourself what other products or services could my customers find valuable. Once you make up a list of those offerings, go out and contact the providers of those offerings and set yourself up as an affiliate and negotiate a referral fee.

Consider a landscaper. As they make their client's lawns and homes into a showcase, those homeowners may also need tree trimming, decking, fencing, stonework, a sprinkler system, outdoor lighting, a patio or outdoor kitchen installed… and perhaps a swimming pool.

The landscaper doesn't perform any of these services, but they are in a prime position to make professional recommendations, and most homeowners will go with those recommendations. The landscaper could easily negotiate anywhere from a 10% to 25% affiliate fee from each of these various service providers, and in the process, double their annual revenue.

I do this myself as a marketing strategist. My top tier clients receive a wide array of additional services I created for them. First, they get complete online access to all of my proprietary marketing and advertising, business growth training, strategies, tactics and resources 24/7/365 through an online E-Learning System I set up.

They receive 2 weekly strategic marketing webinars where I teach them one specific strategy designed to immediately increase their revenue and profits. They gain access to a weekly Application Workshop where I personally help them to take that marketing strategy they just learned and show them how to implement it for their specific business. They also get a weekly Ask The Expert call with me where they can ask me ANY business related question they need answered... and then we meet once a month for an exclusive Mastermind session where we find the group dramatic breakthroughs in both their sales and marketing efforts.

I also host for this group a monthly "lunch and learn"... and I show them how they can get their business ranked on page one of Google. I created all of these additional services offerings myself... so these weren't something I had to go out and purchase. In fact, NONE of these services cost me a cent to develop or implement, but they are extremely attractive to a LOT of small business owners. They also do an excellent job of separating me from all of my competitors, because no one else I know of offers anything even close to what I provide to my clients. My point being that we can do this for YOUR business as well.

How many additional offerings do you estimate you could be making right now? All you need to do is contact each service provider you identify and effectively negotiate a deal with them that's win / win. I would conservatively estimate that this strategy will add an additional 10% of your current total revenue to your bottom line.

In a recent case study, I found $18,000 in additional annual revenue by simply offering additional products and services to their customer base.

$18,000 in additional annual revenue increases the valuation of that business somewhere in the range of $50,000 - $75,000.

Chapter 7
Higher Prices – Bundling

Now let's check out a strategy for our 4th profit formula component… getting higher prices for what you sell. I like to use a "bundling" strategy here.

Bundling is simply the process of grouping together certain products to create 'packages' which are then sold to clients. When you do this, you completely eliminate the biggest complaint small business owners have these days… competing on price.

Bundling removes price from the equation by creating an "apples to oranges" comparison. You have to remember that customers today shop value… NOT PRICE! Unfortunately, small businesses are LOUSY at conveying their "value proposition"… so therefore, price becomes the only value proposition left to consumers.

The real key to success in marketing is to offer more value than your competition. Prospects will pay twice the price if they believe they're receiving four times more value. Unfortunately, most businesses… in a vain attempt to increase their value… begin to offer discounts, and that often destroys their margins. Did you know if some businesses discount their price by a mere 10% they now have to sell 50% more just to break even?

For example, if you sell a widget for $100, and you have a 30% profit margin, you make $30 for every widget you sell. That means your cost basis for that widget is $70. If you discount that widget 10% and sell it for $90 instead of $100, your cost basis is still $70. Now you're only making $20 in profit instead of $30.

For this business to make $1000 in profit selling their widgets at $100 each, they would need to sell 33.3 widgets ($30 X 33.3 widgets = $1000). But by discounting their price 10%, now they need to sell 50 widgets ($20 X 50 widgets = $1000). They now have to sell 50% more widgets just to get back to their original profit margin. (33.3 X 1.5 = 50).

But consider this… when was the last time you saw a business offer a measly 10% discount? Most of the time they offer 20% to 40% discounts… and then they scratch their heads wondering why they're going broke. And to add even more bad news on top of this already bleak scenario, did you know that the latest research shows that discounting doesn't actually impact a prospect's buying decision unless that discount is for 40% or more?

Want to know the closely guarded secret that successful businesses DON'T want you to know?

STOP discounting!!! Instead, innovate your business so you offer more value than your competition… even if that means increasing your price. When you discount your price, you lose the full value of every dollar you discount. Bundling increases the perceived value so prospects buy more.

Consider a home builder or remodeling contractor. They typically contract with certain suppliers that offer them huge volume discounts… especially for electronics. One builder agreed to buy multiple packages of a whole house entertainment and security system including… a 50 inch HDTV, a complete high quality surround sound system, a complete home security system including surveillance cameras at all entry points to the home and a complete fire protection and monitoring system.

The retail price for this package was $22,800 installed... but the builder acquired them in volume for around $6500 since installation would not be part of their costs. Since the builder already has the home stripped to the studs, installation can be handled during the actual project by their crew for pennies on the dollar. Now imagine this builder competing with other builders in a moderately priced neighborhood. All the builders offered homes in the $150,000 price range.

Our builder offered their home for $156,500... which included the additional $6500 out of pocket expense to the builder... and their home comes standard with a $22,800 home entertainment and full security system for FREE! Which builder would you buy from? In fact, what if this builder offered that new home for $160,000? Do you really believe that additional $3500 would prevent anyone from buying this home?

And does it still look like a MUCH better deal than the $150,000 home without the system? If the additional $3500 increase did make a difference due to loan qualification standards for certain prospects, the builder always has the option of reducing the price back to $156,500. They could even maintain their original price of $150,000 and lower their profit margin on each home sold.

This would allow them to possibly double their normal sales volume and practically double their overall profits every year. After all, they're still making around a 30% profit at $150,000. A home remodeler could use this same type of positioning for every remodeling job they bid on. Are you starting to see the potential here? Here's the marketing campaign that was developed for this builder.

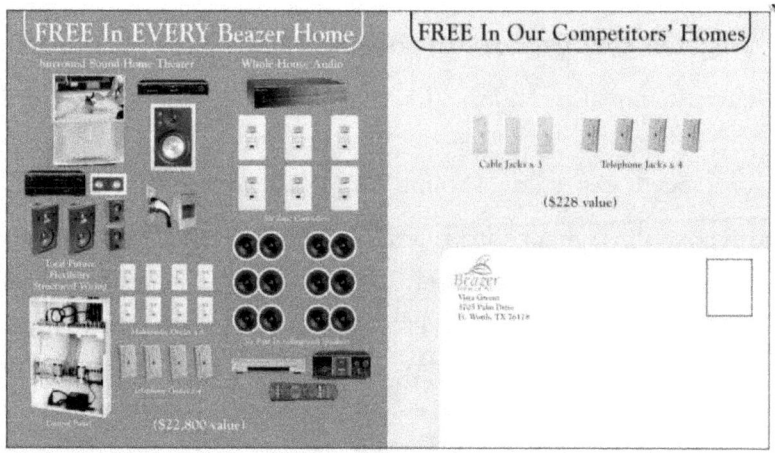

But consider this fact. In the case of the builder, the home security and entertainment system wasn't something they normally dealt with. It wasn't a product they typically carried.

They simply discovered that this was something their prospects wanted to have included in the homes they were purchasing...

so the builder went out and created an affiliate relationship with the home electronics provider and wound up doubling their sales and profits.

You just need to sit down and create a list of all the potential products and services you could bundle for YOUR business. This strategy can add substantial revenue for YOUR business. For the purposes of staying conservative in our estimates, let's do this? Bundling can easily increase any businesses revenue by 25% to 40%. Could we conservatively say that you could easily expect to see a minor 10% revenue increase in your first year of using this strategy? So what does that translate to based on your current annual revenue?

In a recent case study, I found $26,000 in additional annual revenue through a coordinated bundling strategy.

$26,000 in additional annual revenue increases the valuation of that business somewhere in the range of $78,000 - $104,000.

Chapter 8
More Profit – Increase Pricing / Internships

Now let's discuss our final profit formula component – more profit.

Obviously there are 2 major ways to increase your overall profitability… increase revenue or decrease your costs of doing business. Let's discuss increasing your profitability first. How about a really simple strategy – raise your prices. Most small businesses have NEVER raised their prices. That's because they don't know the facts when it comes to increasing their pricing. They're scared to death that ANY price increase, no matter how small, will lead to a mass exodus of all their customers. But is that really true?

Let's say you sell a widget for $100 and decide to increase that price 10% to $110. Will that small increase REALLY lead to a loss of customers? Honestly, I believe a few will leave, but they are most likely your biggest price shoppers that show NO loyalty or patronage to your business anyway. They will beat you down price-wise every chance they get, and the moment you begin to make a decent profit, they will leave you in a heartbeat for the next business willing to accept a financial beat down. But even though there will be some customer attrition… to what extent? Let's look at the numbers.

The business selling this widget is now making an additional $10… ALL of which is pure profit. Right there, that's a 33% profit increase. For this business to make $1000 in profit selling their widgets at $100 each, they would need to sell 33.3 widgets. But by increasing their price 10%, they only need to sell 25 widgets.

That means that just to BREAK EVEN, this business would have to LOSE 25% of its customers over a measly 10% price increase… and that simply ISN'T going to happen!!! Of course, we need to perform a thorough price analysis on your business and determine the most lucrative price increase for you, but this is definitely a strategy I strongly recommend to all of my small business clients to help them increase revenue. There simply is no FASTER or EASIER way to generate additional revenue.

But now let's discuss option two… decrease your costs of doing business. One of the best ways to do this is to cut your labor costs. That's a HUGE expense for any small business. Salary, benefits, social security taxes, unemployment insurance, worker's comp., etc. really add up. And yet, what can you do? You MUST have the labor you need to operate your business… especially as these other strategies we've looked at begin to create exponential growth for your business.

This is where I like to use an "internship" strategy. Instead of hiring new personnel as you grow, consider offering an internship. Go to your local junior college, college or university and offer an internship for the semester or the year to those seeking degrees or experience in a similar field or area of expertise as your business. For example, every business needs additional administrative help, so offer an internship to a student majoring in business administration. The schools LOVE it when a business offers internships since they act as a value-add to their educational offerings by providing their students with real world experience.

The kids LOVE them for several reasons… it gets them OUT of the classroom. After all, 16 years is more than enough as far as the kids are concerned. The kids really do obtain real world experience… and that experience looks great on their resume. It gives them a jump start on their peers when they graduate… especially since the company providing the internship often hires them upon graduating since they're already trained and experienced in their processes.

The employer loves them for obvious reasons – they don't have to pay these kids a salary because the kids receive college credit hours as their compensation. Internships can save small business owners tens of thousands of dollars each year.

Let me ask you a couple of questions. First, let's revisit pricing. Do you think we might be able to increase your pricing by a meager 5% without running into any meaningful attrition? OK, question number two. When would you anticipate needing additional administrative help, keeping in mind that the strategies we've reviewed today have the potential to increase your annual revenues dramatically? How much would you estimate you would have to pay that person, and make sure you include all of the miscellaneous costs associated with hiring an employee?

Record that figure as additional revenue. If you don't anticipate an administrative hiring need in the future, do you see any future need for any type of additional personnel moving forward? If those positions could be filled by an intern, calculate your savings.

In a recent case study, I saved one business owner more than $15,000 in additional annual expenses by offering an internship to a qualified college senior.

$15,000 in additional annual revenue increases the valuation of that business somewhere in the range of $45,000 - $60,000.

Now add up all the revenue you've just identified throughout all 8 of these strategies. Keep in mind that number was arrived at CONSERVATIVELY. And keep in mind this revenue ISN'T a one-time increase... this is revenue you will generate year after year after year... as long as you diligently execute these strategies. But here's the REALLY exciting news. All of this additional revenue we've just discovered... this is a mere drop in the bucket. Let me explain. Do you remember when we started this meeting and I showed you this Profit Growth Calculator?

If you increase each of those 5 profit formula areas by a mere 10% you would see your annual revenue almost double... from $62,500 to over 6 figures.

But if you could increase each of the 5 areas by 50%... your business would skyrocket from $62,500 to almost half a million dollars annually. Most business coaches today work in that 10% range, and to keep today's numbers conservative, that's also the range I've asked you to keep your revenue increases within. But 10% is NOT the ballpark I play in. I play in the 50% and higher ballpark, and I have for many years now.

Can you imagine what your revenues would look like with 50% or higher increases in each of these 5 areas? But I personally think all that additional revenue is secondary... and that there is something far more important at stake here.

When you execute each of these 8 strategies, you've just created a SYSTEM for your business that will generate a CONSISTENT, large number of leads, conversions and sales on an on-going basis. This systemization of your business creates a self-sustaining model that runs on its own... WITHOUT you having to be there yourself. This is where you start to gain not only economic freedom... but also freedom of time. Consider this.

If someone owns a business building websites, every time they deliver a website to a client they have to go out and find a new client. It's never-ending for them. But when you execute these 8 strategies, you will always have new orders in your pipeline thanks to compelling and powerful advertising coupled with your drip campaign. You will have JV's sending you revenue.

You will have upsells, downsells and cross-sells taking place DAILY... along with selling additional affiliate products and services to your customers. You will implement higher pricing that your customers will WILLINGLY pay you... thanks to the higher perceived value you've created. And you will have lower costs that will add significant revenue to your bottom line.

The only thing standing in your way now is getting all of this implemented in a timely and efficient manner. Please let me know if this is something you would like me to help you with?

SPECIAL FREE BONUS GIFT FOR <u>YOU</u>!

To help you achieve more success, there are
FREE BONUS RESOURCES for you at:

MyWealthZone.com

Get your 4 <u>FREE</u> video series and our weekly tips on how to become more entrepreneurial, run your business more efficiently, conduct more effective marketing, and better serve your clients.

FREE $497 VALUE